Peacefully Parenting Through Prana
Heart-Centered Solutions for Families

By: Amy Williams,
Founder of Parenting Through Prana

I write this with immense gratitude and respect for all of the spiritual teachers who have influenced my life. Specifically, to Grand Master Choa Kok Sui the founder of Pranic Healing and Arhatic Yoga, and to Matt Kahn for his revolutionary work in the area of self-love.

Table of Contents

Forward

The primary goal of this book it to begin teaching you, a busy parent, how to readily access and work with your innate love prana in the most practical, simple, easily replicable ways allowing you to flourish as the heart-centered parent you want to be.

You will learn how working with love prana and activating the Heart-Crown Connection is the secret to reprogramming reaction cycles into response patterns within the subconscious mind and how that helps us rewire and sooth our overactive nervous systems so you can actually do the compassion based parenting that feels so right in your soul.

I'll share tips for dealing with some of the personal struggles that led me to this synthesis of energy medicine, spiritual development, self-love, and neuroscience to create a new paradigm within peaceful parenting that breaks through all barriers to make this accessible and functional for every parent.

Learning to follow the prana is the empowerment you've been looking for to take your heart-centered parenting out of the mental knowing and into the your real everyday life where you can truly apply it in the ways you want to.

My heart radiates with gratitude, love, and excitement for you as you begin this book.

The Power of the Heart

The heart-center is one of the most powerful gifts we possess not only as parents but as human beings. Looking at all major religions and philosophies we see heavy emphasis on the importance of the heart. Even science is discovering that there are more neural pathways going from the heart to the brain showing that the heart has more influence on the brain than the brain on the heart. Through my personal experience I have discovered that your heart-center, or heart chakra, is truly your parenting superpower and that the prana of love radiating from this space can not only change your parenting, but change the world.

In so many ways we have been told that love is the answer, only love is real, love is the greatest power on earth, and that is genuinely the simplified truth. However, that doesn't tell us how to access it and use it.

There is ancient wisdom in each of us that has been lost and is now being reseeded throughout our planet. For me, this wisdom has been placed in my heart to help parents understand how love works not just as a feeling or idea. I hope through this book I can create clarity and empowerment around the concept of love.

As parents we influence the entire world by raising the next generation. That is not only a gift but a responsibility to all of humanity.

Society teaches us to focus on our children's performance as a way to gauge our productivity and value as parents so we can decide if we've done a good enough job based on our children's worldly success. As our planet is waking up we're stepping into a time where the collective consciousness of our planet will desire and crave and strive for spirituality to shift this planet into higher states of consciousness. Our children are here to help us do that. They will push us in every way to start creating the world their souls have come here to live in.

Exquisitely enough, we have just the power inside of each of us to give our children exactly what they need. We can do this not just because we are their parents and our souls huddled up and chose to have this adventure together before we all incarnated into these bodies, but because we possess a heart chakra and all of the magnificent blessings and abilities that come with it.

It is through activating what I call the Heart-Crown Connection that we access the ultimate win-win for parents and children. Activating the heart chakra, which I will talk about much more throughout this book, creates a cascade of influences and responses within our entire being. These shifts effect us not just energetically but emotionally, mentally, and physically.

I could spend the rest of my life diagramming and illuminating all of the proofs of these responses and connections that are available through every field of study, but the good news is I won't need to. As you practice Heart-Crown activation you will actually begin to see these connections yourself. They will start to jump out at you from books, and videos, and religious texts as if you were seeing the world with completely new eyes. So rather than spend an immense amount of time writing this like a research paper I'm just going to cover the basics and leave it open for further exploration in whichever direction has peaked your curiosity. Also, I don't want to lose you before we get to the fun part where we apply it in our parenting.

To begin, we need a very basic understanding of the energy body. Each of us is composed of a energy body that is the blueprint for our physical, mental and emotional bodies, or systems. The energy body goes all the way through our physical body and extends outside of it. Within the energy body are chakras which are energy centers. We have some major ones and some minor ones and they all do different things. I highly recommend reading "Miracles Through Pranic Healing" by Master Choa Kok Sui for a detailed undertsnading of the energy body and chakras if you'd like to learn more. For the purpose of this book we are going to focus on the heart and crown major chakras. The heart chakra is located in the center of the chest and the crown is on the top, or crown, of the head.

When the heart chakra is activated, which we will discuss how to do in the following chapters, it naturally activates the crown chakra. The crown chakra is our connection and an entry point within our energy body for divine energy to flow into us. Activating these chakras means that they become larger can hold and process more divine energy. Divine energy contain higher levels of wisdom, intelligence, and compassionate love for the whole or group, also known as oneness consciousness. The crown chakra helps our brains to function properly. As more divine energy enters the crown chakra and the brain we are able to think more clearly, make decisions more easily, and have a higher intuitive knowing of what is right, not just for ourselves but also for the collective, or for our purposes, the family.

Another aspect of activating the heart chakra is that doing so regulates, or brings into balance, the chakras below it. Chakras can get out of balance when they are over or under activated. For example, when we are in high stress situations for prolonged periods of time our solar plexus chakra can get too big and we can feel uncontrollably emotional. This is just one example and it would take books and books to describe all the ways that chakras can be in a less than optimal state. In fact, they have already been written. The focus point for us is that when the heart chakra is activated it automatically balances out and brings a homeostasis to many other chakras, all of which influence how we feel and show up in our lives.

The heart is our center of earthly love. It is where we love places, things, and individuals. So when we stimulate that space we feel happier, calmer, and more joyful. When this happens our whole being is imbued with love prana, or energy, which radiates through and out of us. This energy has a soft, sweet, peaceful transmutational quality. This loving prana combined with the golden divine prana from the crown is our secret sauce for parenting.

That means we can learn how to allow the flow of more divine love prana into our being and direct it to the areas of our family that need it the most.

So now we can see that activating the Heart-Crown Connection has many benefits on the energetic level. It helps us feel better, think better, and brings other parts of our energy body into balance. If the heart chakra is our earthly love and the crown chakra is our divine love then we are not only filled with and radiating our loving prana, we also have put ourselves in a state of alignment with the divine will, or divine plan for all of humanity. This means we have a more cooperative energy as we are begin influenced by a desire to bring harmony and peace at a global level. That energetic, or pranic, influence begins first in our own homes and families and most importantly within ourselves.

This brings us to the concept of self-love. Self-love has been such a buzz word lately and while it can mean bubble baths and general self-care, we are going to approach it from an energetic perspective. The way I teach self-love is as a very real and tangible process. It is the process of activating the Heart-Crown Connection, because as we just discussed this is the way we can imbue and radiate the highest and purest forms of loving prana through us.

To truly love ourselves means we make the decisions that are right for us, we take actions that are healthy and healing for us, from an inner space where we are truly accepted and supported. Activating the Heart-Crown Connection gives us all of this.

In every moment, as Matt Kahn says, we need "more love, not less". Part of the reason this is so true is that when we are in this self-loving state we are in our optimal state. So it does not matter what has happened that makes us think we are unworthy of love, the highest truth is that choosing to consciously generate that love through you will put you in the best pranic, mental, emotional, and physical state to make the right decisions for yourself and your family moving forwards.

In order to have the impact we desire in our family it makes sense that we would chose to be in our optimal state if we have that option, right? Of course it does! To be in that position we have to embrace a state of self-love for it is in this state that we have become channels of the love we wish to share.

A big part of why caregivers get tapped out is that they are not channeling the love prana they need to sustain themselves to continue to give. You've heard the phrase pouring from an empty cup, but did you know that the crown chakra literally opens up like cup or vessel to allow us to hold a greater amount of divine energy? So the cup is literal. When the Heart-Crown Connection is weaker and not activated the cup is smaller and can hold less prana and therefore has less to give. When there is less to give our ability to think and make good judgments is clouded, the peace within us is not as stable, and so forth. Essentially, the benefits of activating the Heart-Crown Connection are not present within us.

It is in giving to our own hearts first, opening the energy channels, and filling our cups first that we are able to create, allow, and receive a sustainable flow of the love prana we need to be compassionate caregivers. It is in giving that we receive.

We tend to think giving and receiving means we get some long-term kick-back but as we activate our Heart-Crown Connection we actually expand our ability to give because we receive first. We give to ourselves first in the way we activate our heart chakra and we immediately receive through the crown chakra.

As we then give to others and continue to give to ourselves we create a beautiful pranic loop that keeps us fully charged and energized because we are no longer giving outwards from a limited supply, but directly connected with the infinite blessings that are already waiting for us to open up to them.

We each have our own current capacity for allowing the flow of love prana, and we can each go so much deeper. All of the great spiritual teachers show us a level of heart-centered existence worthy of imitation. They show us what humans are capable of.

Even as you read these words and your heart hears the truth within them you are already one step closer to parenting through prana.

Notes

<u>Notes</u>

Expansion and Contraction

Now that we have laid the groundwork for understanding what it means to be living from our heart space by activating the Heart-Crown Connection, the question becomes, "how do I know when I am truly connected with my heart-center?".

Unfolding the layers of truth within this discovery will be an ongoing process with deepening understanding as you progress. However, we can measure this for ourselves by calibrating our personal sense of *expansion* and *contraction*.

Let's start with an easy exercise to sensitize ourselves to what expansion and contraction feel like inside of us.

1. ***While in a calm space recall a happy memory, let yourself be filled with the joy and bliss of this moment. It can be as momentous as a marriage or as simple as a clean counter. Any memory that brings you joy is the right one. Let your senses be filled with the sensation of reliving all of it as if you are there right now. You are smiling. Do not rush this experience. It can help to close your eyes. When you feel thoroughly satiated with this glorious moment you are ready to continue reading. What you are experiencing is expansion.***

2. *Now remember something stressful. Did you feel the immediate shift? The tightening feeling? That is contraction.*

This exercise can be repeated as often as you need clarification. When we are in a state of expansion we can literally feel as though we are growing bigger, unfolding, and unfurling into the space around us like a weight has been lifted. Often we were not even aware of this weight until the expansion arose. This expansion is the opening and activation of the heart chakra and the loving energy that radiates out through us into our environment. Likewise, the contraction is just the opposite, it is the pulling in and shrinking away of the heart chakra.

Like a small child who it trying to hide in a corner to protect itself by becoming as small and unnoticeable as possible, we have learned through our experiences and stored in our subconscious a programming that we are safer when we become small. As we learned in the last chapter, quite the opposite is true! It is when our heart center is blossoming with fullness and we are washed in the benefits of our Heart-Crown Connection that we are truly in our optimal state of human being and therefore parenting.

I encourage you to spend time throughout your day simply becoming aware of when you experience a state of expansion and when you are shifting into contraction. Which experiences make it easier to stay in your natural state of openness and which ones trigger a reaction of contraction? You may even like to keep a list to help physicalize your observations for easy reference as we progress.

This exercise is simply for observational purposes at this point. We want to develop our awareness of the world around us and our internal reactions without judging the experience we are having or the outer events that triggered us. Later, we will step into the power of mindfulness and start to reprogram those subconscious, Contraction Reactions Cycles into Expansion Response Patterns.

Notes

Notes

Mindfulness vs Awareness

Now we are going to build on our understanding of expansion and contraction by more thoroughly defining mindfulness and awareness. In our previous exercise we felt the flip-flop from expansion to contraction like the light switch of our heart-center being turned on and off. I asked you to spend time throughout your day developing your awareness by observing which experiences in your routine make it easy to feel expansion and which ones trigger contraction reactions. If you chose to keep a list of some of these moments now would be a good time to have it for reference. If you kept a running mental list or simply observed without cataloging that is okay too.

The words 'mindfulness' and 'awareness' are often used interchangeably, however, I am going to share it with you, the way I understand it, from how it was shared with me, because it has been such a help in unraveling my inner world and making sense of knowing when feelings and thoughts are truly my own, or belonging to the environment around me.

Defining 'Aware' and 'Mindful'

- ***Being aware is recognizing through observation the energies that are outside of you, which you encounter***

- *Being mindful is recognizing through observation which energies are coming from within you, and making a conscious decision about how to respond to them.*

To overly simplify aware means knowing what is outside of you and mindful means knowing what is inside of you and therefore yours to respond to.

Let's do a simple exercise to help you develop a sense of what is yours and what is not.

1. *Take a moment to check in with yourself asking how you are feeling. Bring attention to your thoughts, where you feel your emotions, and any tension in your body.*

2. *Now that you have a baseline to observe from you are going to ask your heart-center a question so you can feel an energetic response. Let this experience be whatever it is, do not try to control it. Some of you will feel a significant difference, while others may only feel it slightly or not at all. That is okay. We are all at different levels of sensitivity. As you continue to connect more deeply with your heart-center your sensitivity will also increase.*

   It can help to close your eyes. Just ask one time and bring attention to the physical, mental, emotional, and energetic response you receive. Sit with this feeling for only a moment.

3. *Now, focus on your heart-center, close your eye,s and simply ask, "do these feelings belong to me or to some one else?"* After a moment **You may observe if there are thoughts and feelings which have lessened and no longer seem as pressing.**

This exercise works for two reasons. The first is that by asking the question we shift out of our solar plexus chakra where a great deal of stress energy is stored and into our will center, or our ajna chakra.

The second, is that by making this shift with a question to your heart you activate your heart chakra into expansion which has a natural balancing and soothing effect on the lower energy centers such as the solar plexus chakra.

The third is that by expanding the heart we get a release, or elevation of loving energy through our entire energy field which can transmute and lessen, or remove, energies which are not so deeply anchored into our energy field i.e. those energies which are new and therefore not belonging to us.

Of course as we learned at the beginning of this book, when we activate the heart chakra the crown chakra follows suit and the benefits include mental clarity and inner peace. This is a way to develop awareness for what is outside of you and triggering a Contraction Reaction Cycle.

What you are still experiencing after this exercise gives you more clarity on what is coming from or attached within you. What is left is where we bring in our mindfulness.

If being mindful is knowing what is within us, what is self-generated or simply unreleased, then mindfulness is the willful and disciplined act of self-reinforcing and self-regulating what is within us. If that feels a bit taxing, scary, overwhelming, or you feel you have already done this and it did not work, stick with me. I'm going to simplify it.

In mindfulness traditions many teach to sit and try to clear the mind until you reach a point of nothingness. That is one way. In my experience and what I have learned throughout my years of spiritual practice it is also a slow way. As a parent, for me, it is an improbable way as hours of silent reflection are impractical for an uncertain outcome. In short, the path of a monk on a mountaintop is unrealistic for a modern day parent. That is why I am here to teach you what I know works.

Once you have spent time observing when you are in expansion and when you are contracting then you know when your Heart-Crown Connection is activated and when it is not. Take a moment, that is a very important sentence.

Logically, we've established that an activated

Heart-Crown Connection is the optimal state for human being, and parenting, as it uplifts and helps regulate us mentally, emotionally, physically, and energetically. It makes sense then, that as we develop an understanding of when we are in expansion and contraction, activation or not, we can apply this activation process to help us with living in mindfulness and awareness.

If mindfulness is consciously reinforcing what we want inside of ourselves, such as choosing expansion, and actively releasing reprogramming that triggers our Contraction Reaction Cycles that cause us to lessen our heart-centered connection, then awareness is knowing when the energy we encounter is not actually our own to deal with. When we develop awareness we also develop compassion for what we are feeling others around us need without sponging it up and treating it as if it is our own.

This single shift into understanding that we can be effected by energy that does not belong to us, and we can learn to identify these moments, and release these energies will be a very deep level of relief for some parents who did not realize how much the energy of their family and environment may be contributing to their dis-ease, or Contraction Reaction Cycle which lessens the activation of their Heart-Crown Connection, and ability to show up to each situation as the parent they truly desire to be.

At this point you are getting a feel for what it

means to experience the expansion of the Heart-Crown Connection within you while developing a sense of awareness for what is outside of you and triggering Contraction Reactions Cycles.

You are starting to understand that mindfulness means consciously choosing to re-enforce, or energetically feed what you want to see grow within you and reprogram what is inside that says you need to contract in order to be safe. And we are learning that activating the Heart-Crown Connection helps us achieve all of this.

Let's take it from conceptual to practical. Whether you have recognized that your outer world is highly triggering Contraction Reactions Cycles within you or you have observed that despite the conditions of your environment your triggers come from within, activating the Heart-Crown Connection shifts us from a state of contraction into expansion no matter what initial factor set off those subconscious programs telling us we are not safe to be open and experiencing the love of our own heart-center.

Practice: Activating Heart-Crown Connection Expansion with "I love you"

1. **Take a moment to tap back into yourself and what you are experiencing in this moment.**

2. *You may close your eyes to bring your mind deeper into yourself for this practice. You can continue with this practice for as long as feels comfortable. With your attention on your heart-center say "I love you".*

Even if you do not feel the genuine expression of these words as you say them, that is okay, keep practicing. It only shows us how much more they are needed. If a wound is bleeding through a bandage we don't say, "oh well, it didn't work", we keep tending the wound until it is stable and healed. For many of us it feels uncomfortable to say "I love you" to ourselves because we never have. This act of saying "I love you" not only activates the Heart-Crown Connection, it also reprograms our subconscious that whatever we are experiencing what we deserve is love. We simultaneously firm our own will that in all moments we choose love. This is consciously, actively choosing expansion, and reprogramming our Contraction Reaction Cycles into heart-centered Expansion Response Patterns. We will continue to learn more about this is upcoming chapters.

There is no benefit to rushing your experience with this activity. You are learning to control the activation of your heart chakra, just as we learn to finely control our physical muscles as they contract and expand.

You cannot go into a gym for the first time and

bench press 400lbs, you will hurt yourself, if you are able to move the weights at all. Your muscles have not been built-up and actively taught how to handle that. Likewise, for most of us our lives have taught us to weaken our hearts by keeping them tightly shut unless the stars have aligned to bring us a perfect moment in which we feel completely safe to love, or we have been moved by a deeper compassion for another.

When we say "I love you" to our hearts it is a way to mindfully lift those energetic and spiritual weights so we become stronger and activation becomes more natural. The first step is not only realizing that you can tap into the power and diving blessing of your natural heart-centered state but actually taking the steps and making the conscious, willful choice to do so.

What we are re-educating our hearts to know is that we are always safe to love and that truly loving, radiating loving prana from our hearts makes us more safe not only energetically, but on all levels.

Why are we more safe? We can think more clearly and our emotions are more balanced so we make better decisions, our physiological responses are what makes our bodies healthy and these become the building blocks to creating and experiencing our lives. Imagine parenting from a space where you feel stable, you can make the decisions you need even if they are hard ones, and your body isn't freaking out while you do it. That feels a lot safer to me. That feeling safer creates a revolving door of heart-centered activation and more free-flowing love prana.

As you move through your days continue to observe when you feel contraction and expansion, to develop awareness by asking "do these feelings belong to me or some one else?", and to mindfully tend to your heart center with "I love you" to activate the Heart-Crown Connection.

Notes

Notes

Feeling Safe

In the last chapter we touched on the importance of feeling safe and how our Contraction Reaction Cycles trigger us to shut down and move us away from the expansion of the Heart-Crown Connection.

In this chapter we are doing to review how a lack of safety triggers our Contraction Reactions Cycles and how we reprogram these into Expansion Response Patterns by freely and consistently tapping into a feeling of safety through our hearts.

As a parent you may have found that there are a lot more things that trigger stress inside of you than you anticipated before having children, or perhaps you were already experiencing stress, worry or anxiety at levels that interfered with your daily life. While this can happen for many reasons, I have found that these experiences are always masking fear and a feeling that we are not safe in that moment. That fear and lack of feeling safe can come in many forms and the reactions can be just as diverse.

The more that I have tapped into the understanding that when I am triggered it is almost always a Contraction Reaction Cycle (CRC's), the easier it has become to work with my heart-center to reprogram these CRC's int o Expansion Response Patterns (ERP's). I have found that it is possible to do this not only during those high-stress situations but even during moments when I am already feeling safe.

I went into more detail about this during the opening chapter so I will keep it more brief and easy to digest here. When we feel unsafe our brains switch out of the conscious space where we make our best decisions and switch to survival mode which puts our brains on autopilot pulling up from the subconscious whatever programs we have learned from earlier in life that will "keep us safe". Those programs may look like yelling, avoiding, self-harming, and much, much more. For almost everyone reading this book, the number one things that this will absolutely look like is contracting the heart-center.

Knowing what we know about how a contracted heart-center effects not only how we feel, but also how our brains and bodies function we can see how logically we're less likely to remember to activate our Heart-Crown Connection while we are under any type of duress. So how can we give ourselves what we need when our brains are in survival mode and we can't remember to do it?

This is why I always tell my clients to practice at low-stakes times. If you want to win a $50,000 basketball shot you don't wait to pick up a ball when you step onto the court to take the shot. You can, but realistically unless you just get lucky you will not perform the way you want to. You practice, practice, practice when you aren't under all of that pressure so that while you are more relaxed you brain and your body are rapidly and joyfully learning how to handle the ball and creating muscle memory. Essentially, over time you need less conscious effort to achieve the same thing that used to take a lot of concentration. The knowledge and practice has created enough neural connections that you can do it on auto-pilot.

Our subconscious is not the enemy it is an subtle instrument that can be finely tuned to reverberate back into us, and the world with whatever we program into it. Most of us have spent the majority of our lives passively sponging up what is around us with less conscious awareness of what was coming in and little mindfulness practice to help reprogram what we let in. I like to explain it like this. When a singing bowl comes under pressure from being struck or the friction of the mallet moves around it the bowl will release, let out, or vibrate into the space with whatever healing frequency it has been made to create. It can't do a high tone if it was made for a low tone. Our brains work under the same principle. When we come under pressure what comes out will depend on our subconscious programming as we will have shifted into survival mode. As we gently retrain our minds through the loving door of the heart what was a Contraction Reaction Cycle can become an Expansion Response Pattern.

Here is how it works. The good news is you have already started! As we speak love to our hearts through the practice of saying "I love you" we teach our heart that it is safe to be open. This activates the Heart-Crown Connection which shifts us out of survival mode and back into a state of consciousness where we are no longer running on autopilot. Every time we choose heart activation we reprogram the subconscious that love is the response to whatever happens.

By doing this consciously and intentionally that Contraction Reaction Cycle shifts and becomes a response pattern of expansion that you have chosen for yourself. Over time that Expansion Response Pattern will override the Contraction Reaction Cycle.

The way it was explained to me is big fish eats small fish. Each of these reaction cycles and response patterns has their own energy. You can think of them as thought fish swimming around in your mind. Which one will get bigger and stronger? The one you feed energetically by repeatedly using it. Which one will rise to the surface when your brain thinks you are in danger? The stronger one.

Saying "I love you" to your heart energetically feeds the thought fish, or thought form, of love within you as an Expansion Response Pattern to whatever comes up in life. The stronger we make this thought form within us by directing the loving prana of our heart to it the bigger it gets. Each time we activate the Heart-Crown Connection the pink loving prana that comes from our hearts imbues our energy field, mental, emotional and physical with this healing light energy that begins to dissipate the thoughts and feelings of fear. So we are feeding the thought forms that we want to become the big fish and lovingly shrinking the ones that we are ready to let fall away and stop popping up as go-to Contraction Reaction Cycles whenever something makes us feel unsafe.

The more often we say "I love you" to our hearts the stronger the energetic heart muscle becomes. What was once heavy to lift becomes easy. Just as we work our physical muscles, it is the same with the heart. You will find it becomes easier to keep your heart open and your Heart-Crown Connection activated the more you practice. That means that during times of duress the Contraction Reaction Cycles that would have before had the power to immediately shut down your flow of loving pink prana will not be as strong anymore as they will have competition with your new Expansion Response Pattern.

We can take this a step further by specifically telling the heart-center you are safe. The more accurate we are in what we say to the being of love in our heart chakra, the more truthful we are within our selves, the more the Heart-Crown Connection is activated and the more loving pick prana can send waves of healing energy through our whole self.

Let's do an exercise to help us feel more safe and create an Expansion Response Pattern of being safe no matter the outside circumstances.

1. *Bring your attention to your heart in the center of your chest. Begin by recalling a happy moment and saying "I love you".*

2. *When you are ready gently think of a recent moment in time when your Contraction Reaction Cycle was engaged. With your focus on your heart repeat "I am safe". Whatever emotions rise up from this moment simply repeat "I am safe".*

You may find a small voice in your mind that seem to tell you that what you are saying is not true and it may offer up compelling evidence.

When we say "I am" we are no longer referring to the body, the thoughts, or the emotions. When we use the words "I am" we energetically engage the higher soul, our divine I AM presence. As we activate the Heart-Crown Connection with the words "I AM" our crown chrakra is flooded with golden healing light and our higher soul, a higher state of consciousness, is able to permeate the mind, emotions, and body elevating us and bring us a little closer to our highest potential.

The more we can create moments of invitation for our highest potential the more rapidly we can convert Contraction Reaction Cycles into Expansion Response Patterns. You will be able to spend increasing amounts of time with an activated Heart-Crown Connection where the abundance of peaceful, loving energy available to you at every moment can flow through yourlife solidifying a sense of safety into your being, no matter what life throws at you.

Notes

Notes

Gratitude is More Than an Attitude

What hasn't been said about it? Who doesn't know they should practice it? Hear me out. Even if you were excited to see this word and think you already have a strong commitment to gratitude I'm going to urge you to read this chapter. I do not want anyone to miss this.

Gratitude is an amplifying energy. Just as love is soothing and calming, the energy of gratitude is so much more than just being glad for what you have.

At the end of the last chapter we began to touch on the power of the crown chakra and our connection to our higher soul consciousness. As we have been learning to activate our Heart-Crown Connection through the heart we have also been activating the crown chakra. Gratitude helps to even further activate the crown which is the channel or cup for receiving divine healing energy. You have heard the saying that you can't pour from an empty cup, but did you know that literally refers to your energetic channels and chakras? Think of it as you cannot give what you cannot receive energetically.

When we are in contraction the cups and channels are smaller. When we activate our Heart-Crown Connection we expand those cups and channels so that more energy can pass through them. Thus, we have more to give and what we give is no longer coming from a finite amount within us as we are more connected to a continuous flow from a higher source.

For example, a tiny stream may dry up during hotter months, but the further downstream you go, where the water ways are wider and faster the more water you will find. If you keep going you will eventually find the ocean where we can never run out of water. It is the same energetically. The more we intentionally activate our Heart-Crown Connection the more we widen and deepen our pranic connection, and the more energy we have, because we are moving closer to the source.

Gratitude is a way of helping to anchor more of the prana we want into out lives by more fully expanding and deepening the cup of our crown chakra so that we may hold more divine loving and healing golden prana.

I'm going to share two ways you can engage with gratitude. If you ever watched "Pollyanna" as a kid then you know how to play the "Glad Game". These practices will be a lot like that. Our subconscious programming can easily lead down a path of looking for and seeing what is wrong. Our brains are magnificent tools. Just like any tool it is all in how you use it. In Pranic Healing we say "the mind is a subtle instrument of the soul", meaning it's there to do the job the soul wants it to do. Unfortunately, through no fault of our own the world we grew up in is full of constant alternative programming from people, music, videos, books, etc all telling our brain how to react to various stimuli.

When we ask our brain why something is happening the brain does what is it told to do. It opens up the filing cabinet and looks for reason for you to be upset or an excuse for why something happened. The brain does not evaluate the truth within this information. It can analyze it for logical connections but it is the heart-center's expansion or contraction that let's us know the level of truth within information.

When we find ourselves asking "why" that's a time when we know we are asking our brains to reach into it's deep dark corners and produce something we already know. We are looking to the past. Gratitude is all about the present and cultivating the future.

When we are triggered as parents we often are not thinking about what our heart-center really needs in that moment to address the situation with loving-kindness. Instead we get lost in the why's. "Why is my child doing this?", "Why can't I figure this out?", "Why isn't this working?", etc. One way that we can effectively step out of "why-ing" is to shift our question from why to what.

Shifting From a "Why" Mindset:

1. **Ask your mind why something is happening. Maybe say *"Why don't my kids listen to me"*. Did you feel your brain start cranking out answers? Did any of them feel good?**

2. Now bring your attention to your heart-center and ask *"what do you need?"*. Make space to sense a response. You can repeat this until you feel a response. As we ask our heart-center to tell us what is needed the Heart-Crown Connection is activates and we begin to feel expansion. What is always needed first is expansion and we achieve that by giving our heart-center our attention. You can even make the question more detailed *"what do you need to feel safe"*.

3. Then give yourself what your heart-center is asking for. No matter how silly or unrelated it may seem. Maybe you hear that you need icecream. It doesn't have to be a lot, maybe it's just one bite to say I heard you heart-center and I am listening. Whatever it is the more you do this in small ways the easier it will become in bigger ways.

In doing this exercise you will connect with the needs of your heart-center, which will shine light on the areas of yourself needing and ready for healing through love prana. When we direct our love it illuminates the darkness that is ready to step into and become part of the light. In this way we are healing parts of ourselves that we are not even aware of before they have to really rise up and have a tantrum to get our attention.

Once you know what you need practicing

gratitude is much easier. Whatever you need is what you will thank your heart-center for and celebrate having it.

Unlike fake-it-till-you-make-it practices we find real validation of the existence of what we want more of and then we create a path for receiving it by giving ourselves more of that prana and reprogramming our subconscious Contraction Reaction Cycle of lack into an Expansion Response Pattern of abundance. In fact we can see from everything I have taught you that there is never anything fake about what you create because it all starts with the prana.

Activating the Heart-Crown Connection Through Saying "Thank You"

1. **Think of something you think you need more of and don't have enough of. Let's use the example of *quiet time*.**

2. **Focus on your heart-center and say *Thank you for so much quiet time"*.**

Your mind may pop up to tell you that this is untrue, there is not "so much" quiet time. But we do have quiet time our focus has just simply been on the noise. Energy flows where attention goes. Between every scream, every block slam, every sudden shriek, or every song, every video, there is a brief moment of silence.

As you cultivate gratitude for, or amplify the prana you want, in these moments of silence you will notice them more frequently. As you notice them more you will appreciate them more, and it will begin to feel as if you have more even though it was always there right in front of you.

You will even begin to have more of the quiet you seek because as you focus on amplifying the quiet through the love of your heart-center then you will be more receptive to receiving more moments. You will also have more quiet within as your Contraction Reaction Cycle is triggered less by noise.

Receptivity means a willingness, or openness, to something. We discussed how our crown chakra literally opens up to receive and hold more divine prana. As we activate our Heart-Crown Connection we become more receptive to the blessings and gifts that are all around us and always available. This is a state of expansion. Expansion equals receptivity. Read that sentence again.

To illustrate this imagine that you are walking down the street overwhelmed with lack and feeling you don't have enough money. You're so consumed, your heart center is in contraction and your receptivity has dropped. You are not looking around at the world seeing opportunity. You don't feel the nudge from your heart center asking you to sit on that bench for a moment, because you have to focus on your money. So you miss the hundred dollar bill lying under the bench, or the opportunity to talk to the person who just sat down and has the perfect job to offer you.

What we focus our minds and energy bodies on is what we will have more of. While many manifestation techniques have people focusing on a far away future outcome the benefit of the gratitude practice is that just like we are filled with love prana when we say *"I love you"*, when we say *"thank you"* we are immediately filled with the prana of having what we want and need right away in that moment and we are more receptive to opportunities to receive it.

We can take this deeper through an elevated form of gratitude, called celebration. Celebration says I have this right now and I am so overjoyed I have to let it out. As you practice gratitude you will naturally come to a place of celebration, but we can also celebrate what we already know is coming and in doing so we bring that prana into us immediately. While this fits the idea of like attracts like, remember that it is really us becoming more receptive to receiving because we are in expansion around that particular energy we've chosen to amplify within ourselves. With our Heart-Crown Connection activated we are in the optimal state to make decisions, choose a loving experience of any situation, and know what is right for us in that moment. That alone is a recipe for success.

To celebrate we do not need to throw a party or involve anyone else at all, but you can. Just like everything else we have worked on up to this point celebration in an internal mechanism that we can do anytime, anywhere.

Applying Gratitude Amplification to Parenting:

1. **Think of something you think is lacking in your parenting or family life. Let's use the example of tidiness. Perhaps you feel your home is not organized or tidy enough.**

2. **Now think of one example in your home of a space that is tidy. It doesn't matter how tidy or how big. Perhaps it is just one drawer in the kitchen, or one pair of shoes put away neatly, one picture hung on the wall, or one toothpaste with the cap on.**

3. **Now say *"congratulations on your tidiness", "congratulations on having the energy and willpower and desire to keep a tidy home (or toothpaste)"*. Continue to repeat it looking for more and more examples.**

Let's do another example. Perhaps you feel your child does not listen well enough. Then instead of continuously directing your energy system at amplifying and affirming that your child does not listen, you can congratulate yourself on having a child who listens so very well because the moment you opened the snack you didn't want to share they heard you and came running. Look for the moments of listening and celebrate them.

Just like with all of the other practices you have learned it is not about WHAT you celebrate is it THAT you celebrate! The prana of celebration is amplifying whatever you put with it.

Another reason that gratitude practice is important is how it interrupts our subconscious programs and helps up rewire our brains and nervous systems for new Expansion Response Patterns.

In Pranic Healing when we talk about the prana of thoughts we say "big fish eats small fish". Your subconscious mind is generally running on auto-pilot at least 95% of the time. That is a lot! That's vastly beyond the majority of your life. What that means is that most of the time we are not in our conscious part of our mind where we actively discern and make new neural connections. We are simply going off of what is already within our minds. Whatever has been programmed into our minds whether through repetition or a strong emotional bond to the information, that is what we are using to move through our daily lives.

But it is not just our minds. When we have thoughts it effects our physical body by the impact it has on our nervous system. So if we have a subconscious program that says loud noises are dangerous and our child starts slamming blocks together, then a signal is sent from the brain to the nervous system saying we are in danger, do something! From there the body will react in the ways that it's neural pathways are most used to or that have been most successfully programmed into it. That can be trying to escape, anger, or becoming overly compensating to appease others. There are many Contraction Reactions Cycles.

As the body reacts the heart rate can go up, and we can get tension in our muscles as we prepare to flee, and so forth. This could be discussed in infinite detail and there are vastly more scientific and detailed explanations available about the physiology of the body in reaction to stress, but for the purpose of this book, you are getting the picture.

When we choose to move through ourselves the prana of celebration, thanks, and love, we reprogram our subconscious and the entire Contraction Reaction Cycle by interrupting it and choosing a new input, an Expansion Response Pattern. That new input has to be either repeated and reinforced or it has to come with a big emotion that strongly anchors it in the mind. Whichever thoughts or programs we "feed" with our energy become the dominant program. This is where the saying "big fish eats small fish" comes in.

We have subconscious programs that are very strongly anchored and have been reinforced for many years. These are the big fish. When we introduce a new Expansion Response Pattern to interrupt the Contraction

Reaction Cycle it comes in as a small fish. Much like fish in a lake the big fish will just eat the small fish. We have to feed it and take care of it and reinforce it. As we do this we are removing the energy we used to put towards keeping the big fish strong.

The good things about the big fish eating the small fish is that each time it does the big fish, or the subconscious program we want to change, is actually consuming it's own healing. The new program, or small fish is a being of love and light sent from the heart center to transmute the negative energies of the big fish and make space for the Expansion Response Pattern you are cultivating.

The Contraction Reaction Cycles we have were created as a form of self-preservation. At some point a message was received within the subconscious that when X thing happens a Y reaction will keep you safe. Until the parts that were initially injured within us are healed through our own love prana amplified by the activation of the Heart-Crown Connection and directed by our mindful attention through love prana these Contraction Reaction Cycles will continue to play out when these self-protective programs are triggered.

As we say "I love", "I am safe", "Congratulation" in response to the triggered program we step into expansion, activate the benefits of the Heart-Crown Connection, and we interrupt the Contraction Reaction Cycle to greet the trauma program with love, gratitude, and safety.

What we essentially say to ourselves and do with our energy body is whatever is showing us needs healed we response with the healing energy of love. Whether we choose "thank you", or "I am safe", or "I love the one", each of these phrases combined with the attention on the heart center is actually an act of self-love because it activates the expansion of the Heart-Crown Connection, which then imbues us with the divine blessing, wisdom, and prana of love through our entire being.

The response is always love prana. The words give a direction and power of concentration towards the area within ourselves that we are now aware needs this love and support to heal. It's like inner talk therapy that reaches right inside of the pain you are identifying and heals it with exactly what it needs, when it needs it 24/7.

Transmutation of these traumas takes time and practice. Remember, big fish eats small fish. Each moment we choose to respond with the activation of our Heart-Crown Connection we program our subconscious with "I love", the prana of love directed from our I AM presence, or our higher souls, and we nourish this as our new Expansion Response Pattern.

As we continue to heal our Contraction Reaction Cycles and reinforce our Expansion Response Patterns we will find that those thoughts, emotions, and behaviors which we wanted to change act out less and less and because they no longer shout so loudly for our attention in order to receive the love they need to rejoin the light within us. We rejoice in gratitude for each little bit of healing that comes to us as we return to our optimal state, one mindful response of expansion at a time.

<u>Notes</u>

Notes

Discipline and Boundaries

In this chapter I am going to pull everything we've learned together and give you examples of how to use these Heart-Crown activations in real parenting situations.

Discipline

I chose to start with discipline because one concern I see so often is worrying that if you become too heart-centered your children will not have structure and order and life will be chaos. So I'm going to calm this belief.

In my personal experience there is nothing self-loving about chaos or a lack of structure to one's day and tasks. It creates an inner turmoil and things are forgotten and left undone that are important to the well-being of oneself and others. This is in no way a criticism for anyone who finds themselves in this space at this point in life. All I am suggesting is that if you engage in a lifestyle where you are fostering a devoted relationship with your heart-center and that relationship provides the benefit of being able to make better choices for you and your family then it is highly unlikely that you will make choices that make your own life more difficult unless it is a growing pain towards the life you want.

When it comes to disciplining children I must first

start by reminding you that discipline comes from the word disciple. It does not, nor has it ever actually meant to create a judgment and punishment to keep a child obedient.   I know you aren't here for that anyways, but it is a common subconscious program that many of us on a path towards peacefully parenting through prana will struggle with. To discipline means to teach and lead by example. As Rudolf Steiner says "be worthy of imitation".

So how do we become worthy of imitation? What do we do when we feel the urge to punish rather than discipline?

When we are looking to change others that is a big red flashing light that we are at an opportunity for self-love. To teach discipline in a way that creates true inner discipline, or mindfulness, we must first be that within ourselves. The discipline you seek is not from another person but for you to be more committed to and mindful of your decision to choose self-love, heart-crown activation, to show up to that situation in your optimal state to handle it.

How to Apply This:

For example, let's say a child does not pick up their toys even though this is an age-appropriate task for them and you feel the urge to change the child and it is not coming out in a healthy way.

Without the Heart-Crown Connection activated you are stuck in contraction and working from your Contraction Reaction Cycle, whatever that may be. For some it is rage, others it may be guilt, yelling, or some others punishment, etc.

Now let's activate the Heart-Crown Connection together to step into expansion and support the response patterns we want to create.

1. **Focus on your heart-center, breathe deeply, and say *"I love you"* several times.**

2. **Take a moment to tap into how you are feeling. With the focus still on your heart center say *"I love the one who is...(insert feelings and be truthful and specific)."* Perhaps you need to say something like *"I love the one who regrets buying those toys"*, or *"letting them into our home"*, *"I love the one who does not want to tell my child to pick up their toys again"*, or *"I love the one who wants to throw all of these toys away and never see them again"*. These are just examples.**

3. **If you are experiencing a great deal of anger perhaps what needs to be addressed are fears underneath. Try saying *"I love the one who is afraid that my child will never pick up their toys like I need them to and I will be stuck having this fight forever and I will lose my my mind"*.**

68

It's good to give yourself a chuckle when speaking to your heart. That's just a sign that it is helping and the heart is expanding.

4. We can further address underlying fears of danger which may be leftover subconscious programs around this type of situation by saying *"I am safe", "I am safe for the toys to be a mess", "I am safe even if my child does not listen to me and pick up their toys when I want them to".* And because we feel we are in danger we often transfer this to our children so you can say *"my child (or insert name) is safe for the toys to be a mess, "My child is safe even if they do not listen to me and pick up their toys when I want them to".*

5. Hopefully, if you have done all of these your breathing is easier and you can smile a bit. This is a good time to practice gratitude. With your attention on your heart-center say *"thank you for such an abundance of toys to fill my home and entertain my child", "thank you that my child has had so much fun in this space", "thank you that I can provide my child with the space and resources to experience so much imaginative play".* After saying thank you we can recognize the blessing of what we have and amplify what we want in our lives by saying *"Congratulations on your abundance!", "Congratulations on having more than you*

need!", "CONGRATULATIONS on being able to provide so well for your child!", "Congratulations on having enough space to hold so many toys".

These are just some ideas to inspire you. You can keep going deeper with each of them to really allow the love prana to flow into whatever area you are experiencing discomfort.

Now that you have chosen to be disciplined in your self-love you ask your heart-center *"what do I need to handle this situation properly?"*. Perhaps it is better storage or a new system of organizing and putting the toys away. Maybe you need to remove toys from your home or from where children can access them. Maybe you need to set a very clear boundary with people who bring toys into your home. Maybe that some one is...you?

Perhaps while doing your "I love You's" you found that you are using the accumulation of stuff to avoid or compensate for other emotions like guilt or fear of missing out. Perhaps you now see that you need to practice this self-love more often so that when it is time to tidy up you are ready to help your child rather than only give a verbal reminder. If any of these "perhaps" felt like contraction then you now know where else you are ready to send your love prana for healing.

When it comes to "stuff" one things that has been

very helpful in my family is to recognize the energetic impact it has on us. Clutter can create a great deal of psychological pressure. When I speak to my children we discuss and view our things as responsibilities. Each item belonging to each person is now a responsibility that they have taken on. We frequently review if the responsibilities are appropriate for them or if they have taken on too much. When new things enter our home we evaluate whether or not we want and can handle the responsibility of taking care of it.

We do not ask if we want it as the primary determining factor, but we ask how it makes our hearts feel thinking about having it, and how our hearts feel thinking about taking care of it. We consider the way it will feel if we spend our money on it and then find we cannot take care of it and have to re-evaluate our other things to decide where to cut down on our responsibilities. Through this practice we observe how our hearts react. Whether it is contraction or expansion helps us decide.

In this way we can help our children create the inner discipline of listening to and working with their heart-center to know what is healthy for themselves so we have less work to do as the enforcer of rules. As children learn to listen to their own hearts and hear their own needs they are more capable of hearing and discerning the needs of others.

Speaking of enforcing rules, if you set a rule then you have to be disciplined enough to follow through for yourself and for them. Whenever we find a rule is not working it is okay to change it for something that works better for everyone. To create more discipline around following family rules you can use the Heart-Crown Connection to help you be disciplined enough to show up to each moment of teaching from your heart-center. That will be the quickest, most peaceful, and harmonious way to help children follow through on household or other responsibilities.

When you are coming from your heart-center you will be able to optimally evaluate whether or not the rule is right, if it needs to be adjusted to meet yours or your child's needs, and how to test out and make changes from a space of collaboration and cooperation, not fear and control.

Boundaries

I firmly believe that much like discipline is really an inner process, the only boundary you will ever need is self-love through activating the Heart-Crown Connection. Here's why:

When you have a strong, healthy relationship with your heart-center you know what is right for you and you have the will to follow through on it without being hindered by subconscious programming such as guilt, trauma from abuse, fear of missing out, etc. The more we consciously and actively choose to participate in self-love, as defined in this book, the more we actually activate another chakra, our ajna chakra, or will center.

We actually develop a stronger will to take the actions we need to simply by activating the Heart-Crown Connection in the ways I've taught you. Essentially, you become more disciplined and mindful about the people, situations, and circumstances around you.

With children this may look like making a shift from feeling very badly about removing toys that are a constant struggle and mess and too much responsibility for them, to recognizing that the situation is unhealthy for you and impacting your ability to show up as a heart-centered parent. You may start to recognize that more harm is done by having a daily fight about the toys for years on end rather than giving yourself an opportunity to experience life without the clutter and stress.

Only you are with you 24 hours a day, 7 days a week to know exactly what you need and how you need it. Only you know what is best for you at all times. Practicing activating the Heart-Crown Connection helps you hear the wisdom of your heart-center more clearly so you can provide for those needs without relying on someone or something outside of you to do it for you. When we are in that empowered state it is easier to identify when a person or situation is not right for you and to avoid the entanglements that often lead us to needing to set boundaries because we didn't listen to our heart-center in the first place. The only boundary is whether or not it creates expansion or contraction within your heart. Expansion is a yes, contraction is a no.

You may be wondering how you can really fully know whether or not the answer is yes or no? Yes is always a YESSSSSS!!! If it doesn't feel like the best thing you've ever thought of then it's a "no". Maybe is a "no". The answer is "no" until you feel the fireworks and certainty of "yes". This can change at any moment, but we wait for the confirmation of our heart expansion to guide the way.

Notes

Notes

Letting Go of Daily Stressors

You know those constant, daily repeated stressors that you really cannot get rid of? The ones that you wake up every morning knowing you will have to deal with no matter how hard you try to avoid it?

This brings us to the topic of forgiveness. Ah, forgiveness can be such a loaded word. Being raised as a Lutheran that word was ingrained into me from a very young age. For a long time I thought that forgiveness meant that you just keep taking it with a smile on your face and then you work really hard to not let it bother you and if it still bothers you then it's your fault because you didn't forgive enough. Maybe that feels familiar?

The true meaning and *functional* pranic use of forgiveness is often hidden. What do I mean by functional? I mean it actually works! Going through this act creates a genuine release from the ties that bind you in anger, hatred, resentment, grudges and all things unforgiveness.

When we forgive successfully what is actually happening is the pranic cord that is connecting us with the person we feel has caused us harm is dissolved. This cord if left intact will continue to fuel and feed the negative prana being exchanged between two people. Every thought and feeling associated with the other person binds the cord tighter, essentially holding both as a pranic prisoner. Forgiveness is freedom from this bondage and therefore the most loving thing we can do for ourselves regardless of the other person. Remember, at all times you deserve to be imbued with and radiating love prana. Choosing contraction because of some one else's actions denies and hurts us first as we slow the flow of our divine gifts that put us in an optimal state for living and parenting.

Forgiveness is freedom from this contraction bondage and therefore the most loving thing we can do for ourselves regardless of the other person. You deserve expansion!

As a parent you want to be functioning at full capacity. With a negative cord like that draining your energy body it's like a hole in a boat. Even if it is small and "manageable" it can eventually sink you and takes constant maintenance if not patched up. The most self-loving action you can take is to activate the Heart-Crown Connection to break these bonds that are depleting your prana. All the prana wasted and lost in not forgiving could be used to propel you forward in life rather than tying you to the past.

The way it is taught in Pranic Healing by my teacher spiritual Grand Master Choa Kok Sui is that there are two kinds of forgiveness. There is inner forgiveness and outer forgiveness.

Inner forgiveness is what we do to free ourselves and others from lower vibrational energy that is binding us together in a harmful way. Outer forgiveness means we allow the circumstances to continue. We can have inner forgiveness without giving another opportunity for the same things to happen again. We can forgive and not forget. When we forget we lose the lesson and have to keep repeating it. Forgiveness says I love myself enough to not make myself keep going through this.

How does this help us in parenting? Have you ever found yourself saying things like *"I've told you a hundred times"*, *"If I have to say it again..."*, *"I can't take this anymore"*? This is a sign that we are still carrying around old hurts and pains from past experiences. We are not in that moment approaching helping our child tidy up their toys the way we did the first time with patience, love, compassion and a willingness to teach. We are still holding on to the other hundred, ok, thousand, times we have asked them before and it didn't go the way we had hoped.

Most parents find it very surprising to recognize how much they are still holding on to towards their children, even tiny children or babies. By letting go of this pranic clutter we can open up healthier, cleaner pathways of between us and our children. We begin with inner forgiveness: first for ourselves, and then for our children through the technique later in this chapter.

Deciding whether or not to have outer forgiveness for a situation involving your children ties back into what we have discussed on discipline and boundaries. Connect with your heart-center and ask what the situation needs, what you need, and what your child needs. Only you know what is best for all of you.

Many of our daily stresses within our family are actually much harder because of a lack of forgiveness more so than the problem itself. That same shoe in front of the doorway, the knock on the bathroom door when you just need a minute, the dish in the sink when you just finished cleaning, and so on. While these things all by themselves are not generally super stressful events, the accumulation of this repeated event or all of these events together in little frequent doses energetically piles up. We know in our minds that it's not that big of a deal and we may even realize that we could more easily take care of it ourselves than involve another person, but we've reached a point where the sympathetic nervous system is in control, our brains are no longer thinking logically, and our solar plexus is heavy with stress.

At this point we need our heart-center to activate to help us begin to regulate ourselves. By giving ourselves the love we need in that moment we can begin to self-sooth and forgive ourselves and others for the events that led up to this moment.

Here's where forgiveness comes in. I like to think of it like a cleaning schedule. There are those things you clean up when the mess happens like spilled milk. Then you have you have those things that just need done regularly because despite your best efforts they keep coming back, like laundry or dirty hand prints on doors. Just like our space need tidying and cleaning so do our pranic, emotional, and mental bodies. That's where we use a practice of consciously releasing to let go of the day's events and make a clean slate for tomorrow. I like to do the following pranic release at bed time.

Forgiveness for Yourself:

1. **Close your eyes and bring your attention to you heart-center and say *"I love you"* until you feel the expansion.**

2. **Visualize yourself in front of you (about a foot tall).**

3. **Say *"I love you, I am sorry for the ways that I have hurt you. I forgive you for the ways that you have hurt me. We all have lessons to learn. I am learning too. I love you, I forgive you, please forgive me."***

4. **Picture a cord connecting you to the image of yourself and say *"You are forgiven. blessings and peace be with you and with me.***

5. **See yourself cutting this cord say *"cut, cut, cut, go in peace"*. Do not worry you cannot damage your connection to yourself. Healthy cords of love always remain.**

6. Take a deep *breath in* moving the prana from your heart-center up, up, up to your crown and *exhale*. Give all of this over to a higher power.

7. Say *"thank you"*.

8. Picture yourself happy.

9. You can repeat this three times for a more thorough cleaning, but if you do not have the time or are not ready then you can move on to forgiving your child(ren).

Forgiveness For Your Child(ren):

• Close your eyes and bring your attention to your heart-center and say *"I love you"* until you feel the expansion.

• Visualize your child in front of you (about a foot tall).

• Say *"I love you, I am sorry for the ways that I have hurt you. I forgive you for the ways that you have hurt me. We all have lessons to learn. I am learning too. I love you, I forgive you, please forgive me."*

• Picture a cord connecting you to the image of your child and say *"You are forgiven. blessings and peace be with you and with me.*

- *See* yourself cutting this cord say *"cut, cut, cut, go in peace"*. Do not worry you cannot damage your connection to people you love. Healthy cords of love always remain.

- Take a deep *breath in* moving the prana from your heart-center up, up, up to your crown and *exhale*. Give all of this over to a higher power.

- Say *"thank you"*.

- Picture yourself happy.

- You can repeat this three times for a more thorough cleaning, but if you do not have the time or are not ready then you can just do it one time.

This first time I used Functional Forgiveness for myself and my children I was amazed at how much lighter I felt.

I know it can be challenging to receive the full benefit of a practice like this through reading. Once it is memorized and becomes part of your regular routine it is a breeze to take a moment when challenges arise and use this as a sort of Rescue Remedy to do a quick cleaning for the situation wiping away the dirty pranic clutter and freeing everyone involved before it has time to really anchor into any of you.

Personally, I always giggle to myself when I'm reading something that begins with "close your eyes". So I have created recordings of forgiveness meditations available on my website to help make it easier to do this practice regularly and even to bring this into your home as a Family Forgiveness Circle.

<u>*Notes*</u>

<u>*Notes*</u>

Yelling

Let's look at yelling from an pranic standpoint: a loss of self-regulation in which a large amount of dirty energy is verbally directed from one person to another.

Oh sure, there is the yelling of spontaneous joy, but I don't think you are reading this because that is a problem for you. The yelling discussed here is the emotional vomiting that has become part of our subconscious Contraction Reaction Cycle as our way to feel safe when we are stressed, angry, scared, etc If you are yelling for any other reason that is not negatively charged then this is not for you, and congratulations on all of your joy!

At a pranic level it is clear that directing negative, dirty, low emotional energy at anyone is a clear symptom of being in contraction and needing expansion through activation of the Heart-Crown Connection.

Remember, prana has to move through you before reaching another person, dirtying your energy body and chakras. Have you ever gotten a sore throat or cough after shouting hurtful things? Do the words ever get choked up as they come out?

Yelling is actually a secondary act of self-destruction & sabotage, a refusal or inability to love through oneself, aka choose expansion, in that moment & then allowing that to spill out onto those around us.

We have not been mindful of the contraction and expansion of our heart in that situation and are trapped in our Contraction Reaction Cycle until we choose to activate our Heart-Crown Connection and affirm our own safety so we can speak with truth. We have all been there, and now we are here learning to change it.

I read somewhere that we yell to reach across the gulf that formed between our hearts. As our heart-centers contract, pull away, and shrink we feel the distance grow between us and the other person. This makes sense when parents and their children are in high stress states. We have been taught through our experiences that we are safer if we contract. Get small to be less of a target and be less noticeable. This is actually a technique in psychic self-defense, to tighten or pull in and contract the energy body to make it tighter and less penetrable. Children often know how to do this protective act intuitively and will cross their arms in front of them which has a closing effect on the aura of the energy body.

It is good because they receive less dirty energy from whoever is yelling. However, this is the last things that we want to happen when we are trying to openly communicate in a family and reach our child so they can understand. So we have to evaluate how our communication is causing this to happen.

We can remember that seeing our children shutting down when we speak is a clear indicator that we need to activate our Heart-Crown Connection and step into the expansion that helps us think and communicate more clearly and through love.

We want to reprogram this Contraction Reaction Cycle into an Expansion Response Pattern that knows the truth; that we are safer the stronger and more expanded we are in our hearts.

Thankfully, the damage can be remedied. The sooner it is addressed the sooner & easier the healing can happen. Think of it like a spill on a white clothe. If you rinse it right away, and you let it soak then you have less chance of the garment being stained. Even if it is still slightly discolored it will be far less than if the stain had had time to really set. After yelling, if attempts are made to erase the energetic damage quickly, then it is not yet as deeply anchored as it will be if it is not transmuted for days, weeks, months, years...

Healing the Trauma of Yelling:

1. **Activate your Heart-Crown Connection through the *"I love you's"* being honest and truthful with yourself about everything you feel in this moment.**

2. **Affirm that you and your child are safe; safe even when people raise their voices and say hurtful things; safe to take time, to take space before addressing this situation further.**

3. **Forgive yourself and your child.**

4. **While it may not feel like a moment for gratitude now is a perfect moment for the prana of being grateful to amplify what you want within you. You can say *"thank you for calmly and clearly communicating"* (you aren't yelling all of the time, right?). *"congratulations on your extensive vocabulary", "congratulations on knowing the right things to say and when to give space to help every situation". Again, these are only examples. If you are struggling to find the words and would like help, I encourage you to work with me to address your specific situations.***

The more you can mindfully activate your Heart-Crown Connection and reprogram the subconscious Contraction Reaction Cycles that have you yelling the sooner you can create an Expansion Response Pattern of honest communication between you and your heart-center. When you can listen and speak with love to your heart that is the communication that will radiate through and out of you.

If you or a family member needs help erasing and mending the damage done by yelling contact me. We can set up a one-one-one session and get at the root of the issues reprogramming Contraction Reactions Cycles into Expansion Response Patterns and creating relief at a cellular level.

Notes

Notes

Making it Work in Day-to-Day Life

By this point you have learned and experienced the power of the following four fundamental principles to accessing the inner wisdom of your heart and how to begin allowing the flow of love prana in each moment. You've worked with simple, practical ways to reprogram you Contraction Reaction Cycles into Expansion Response Patterns as you develop your awareness and strengthen your will to mindfully activate your Heart-Crown Connection. Let's review.

Fundamental Principles:

- In every moment we are either choosing contraction or expansion of our heart-centers. We have the power to choose how we experience the situations that arise in our parenting.

- Feelings arise to show us where we need more love prana to flow and to tell us we are ready to do so. Each trigger and realization that we are in contraction is an opportunity for heart-centered expansion.

- When we activate our Heart-Crown Connection we send loving prana to parts of ourselves that are ready to heal.

- As we shine the light of our love prana into the spaces ready to heal we create a cascade of healing through all parts of us by interrupting our Contraction Reaction Cycles and creating new Expansion Response Patterns that ripple through our subconscious minds and physical bodies calming down our overactive nervous systems.

Applying These Principles

Your number one focus in each moment is recognizing and observing without judgment where you are feeling contraction and actively choosing to allow expansion by activating the Heart-Crown Connection. You choose expansion because in every moment you deserve more loving divine energy no matter what the circumstances or people involved. You can activate the Heart-Crown Connection and use your love prana to reprogram Contraction Reaction Cycles into Expansion Response Patterns in the following ways:

- Always begin with saying *"I love you"* to your heart-center and specifically directing loving prana to the areas that are calling for it. *It doesn't matter what you love, it matters that you actively direct the flow of love prana.*

- When you feel anger, impatience, fear, and other uncomfortable energies-in-motion it is an opportunity to re-educate your energetic, emotional, mental, and emotional bodies that you are safe. As you feel safe you can clearly identify how to appropriately respond to the situation. Focus on your heart and say *"I AM safe"* and continue to clearly identify the triggers and that you (and your children) are safe. *It doesn't matter what you are safe from or how you are safe, it matters that you feel (are filled with the energy of) safe.*

- Gratitude is our proactive way to flow in expansion and activate the Heart-Crown Connection without relying on an uncomfortable experience to do so. It can also be an Expansion Response Pattern to triggers, when we are ready to take that step. Gratitude can be applied through a conscious act of celebration. Focus on your heart-center and say "Congratulations on your abundance". Continue to look for evidence of abundance around you and congratulate yourself on having it. *It doesn't matter what you celebrate, it matters that you celebrate.*

- Giving and receiving love prana is an ongoing ever-flowing process. It is not linear. As we give we receive, as we receive we give because it flows out of us into our environment. As we take these intentional actions towards cultivating our Heart-Crown Connection we allow ourselves to be in that state of flow rather than caught in the trap of filling our cup only when we see we've emptied our cup. It's the difference between a fountain that is circulating water and a hose that is turned on and off again.

It does not matter as much which way you choose to apply these principles so much as it matters that you do choose expansion in some way. These methods are simple guided ways you can seize the potential in every moment as an opportunity to shift into expansion.

As you practice mindfully choosing expansion through activating the Heart-Crown Connection your world will begin to change. The energetic clutter that once prevented you from clearly knowing what to do and feeling safe doing it will begin to fade away as the trauma that led to it's development as a protective mechanism is healed. However, this is just the beginning of what is possible.

Activating the Heart-Crown Connection to direct the flow of loving prana can be applied in untold ways because it is our birth right and our natural state. I regularly work one-on-one and in groups with parents to help them personalize this practice for their specific situations and needs. I create a heart-centered, judgement-free, safe space for sharing triggers and practical ways to create the expansion parents desire. If working with me feels good in your heart-center you can follow my contact information at the end of the book under "Work With Amy". I also have resources and guidance courses available on my website and in my online parenting group. I invite you to follow me on social media. All of this information is in the next section of this book.

Thank you so much for investing in yourself and your family through this book and the practices it shares. Your choice to chose expansion not only uplifts yourself and your family, the love of your radiant heart ripples out into the entire world around you bringing more light, love, and power to every being on the planet. May you be blessed with the will to practice regularly. With an overflowing heart-center I end this book and look forwards to connecting with you in my community space and working together one-on-one. Thank you!

Notes

Notes

Work With Amy

Hello! Thank you so much for taking the time to read this book. I know the divine loving prana it contains will continue to digest and and expand within you in unimaginable ways.

I'd like to personally invite you to join me in my online community *"Parenting Through Prana with Amy Williams"* where we learn more about activating the Heart-Crown Connection to shift daily challenges into a heart-centered win-win for parents and children.

I highly encourage you to deepen your expansion by working with me. I offer one-on-one sessions and very soon this book will be the foundation of an online offering where I can answer your questions live. Through Pranic Healing we will rapidly accelerate the disintegration of old Contraction Reaction Cycles and enhance the cellular uptake of new Expansion Response Patterns.

I welcome you to my website where you can find a variety of heart-centered resources and courses for parents and children.

Peacefully Parenting Through Prana:
Heart-centered Solutions for Families

Author: Amy Williams,
Founder Parenting Through Prana

ISBN: 9798476449034

Text copyright 2021 by Amy Williams

Printed in Great Britain
by Amazon

76866542R20061